FAMOUS
ATHLETES

# MIKE TROUT

by Tracy Nelson Maurer

Gail Saunders-Smith, PhD, Consulting Editor

Pebble® Plus

CAPSTONE PRESS
a capstone

Pebble Plus is published by Capstone Press,
1710 Roe Crest Drive, North Mankato, Minnesota 56003
www.capstonepub.com

**Library of Congress Cataloging-in-Publication Data**
Maurer, Tracy, 1965–
  Mike Trout / by Tracy Nelson Maurer.
     pages cm.—(Pebble plus. Famous athletes)
  Includes bibliographical references and index.
  ISBN 978-1-4914-6237-9 (library binding : alk. paper)—ISBN 978-1-4914-6253-9 (ebook pdf)—
ISBN 978-1-4914-6257-7 (pebble books pbk. : alk. paper)
1.  Trout, Mike, 1991– —Juvenile literature. 2.  Baseball players—United States—Biography—
Juvenile literature.  I. Title.
  GV865.T73M38 2016
  796.357092—dc23
  [B]                                                                          2015001900

**Editorial Credits**
Erika L. Shores, editor; Juliette Peters, designer; Eric Gohl, media researcher;
Lori Barbeau, production specialist

**Photo Credits**
AP Photo: Rich Schultz, 13; Courtesy of The Press of Atlantic City: Michael Ein, 9, 11;
Dreamstime: Scott Anderson, 7; Newscom: Cal Sport Media/David Hood, 15, Cal Sport Media/
John Mersits, cover, Cal Sport Media/Peter Joneleit, 1, 22, Icon SMI/John Cordes, 5, Icon SMI/
Rich Graessle, 19, UPI/John Angelillo, 17, USA Today Sports/Jesse Johnson, 21

Design Elements: Shutterstock

## Note to Parents and Teachers

The Famous Athletes set supports national curriculum standards for social studies
related to people, places, and culture. This book describes and illustrates Mike Trout.
The images support early readers in understanding the text. The repetition of words
and phrases helps early readers learn new words. This book also introduces early
readers to subject-specific vocabulary words, which are defined in the Glossary
section. Early readers may need assistance to read some words and to use the Table of
Contents, Glossary, Read More, Internet Sites, Critical Thinking Using the Common
Core, and Index sections of the book.

Printed in the United States of America in North Mankato, Minnesota.
042015          008823CGF15

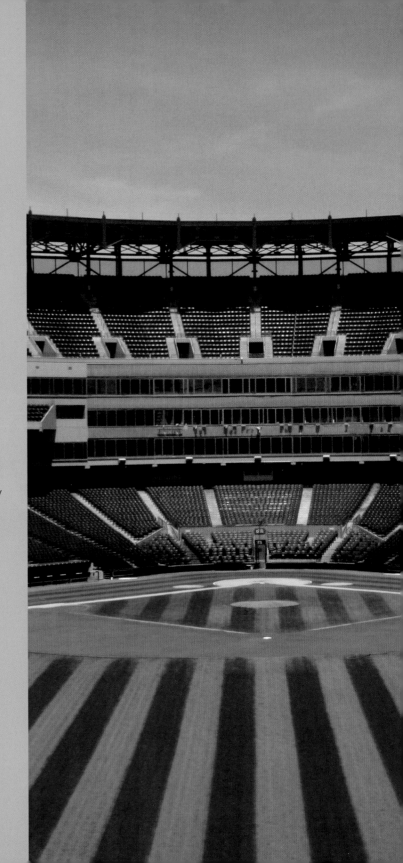

# TABLE OF CONTENTS

# A BASEBALL FAMILY

Michael Nelson Trout was born
August 7, 1991. He grew up
in a baseball family.
Mike learned from his father,
Jeff Trout. Jeff had played
minor league baseball.

**1991**

born in
Vineland,
New Jersey

Mike Trout in 2014

As a child Mike often slept

in his tee-ball uniform.

In Little League he wore

#2 on his shirt. It was

the number his favorite player,

Derek Jeter, wore.

born in
Vineland,
New Jersey

Derek Jeter played for the New York Yankees.

# HIGH SCHOOL STAR

Mike played baseball at

Millville Senior High School

in New Jersey.

He was a good pitcher

and hitter. But his coaches

liked his speed best.

**1991**

born in
Vineland,
New Jersey

**2007–2009**

attends high
school in Millville,
New Jersey

In 12th grade Mike moved

to play in the outfield.

He hit 18 home runs that year.

It set a high school record

in New Jersey.

born in
Vineland,
New Jersey

attends high
school in Millville,
New Jersey

11

# MLB SUPERSTAR

People thought Mike would
be picked early in the 2009
MLB Draft. But 24 other players
were drafted before him.
Finally the Los Angeles Angels
of Anaheim chose Mike.

MLB stands for
Major League Baseball.

**1991**

born in
Vineland,
New Jersey

**2007–2009**

attends high
school in Millville,
New Jersey

**2009**

drafted by the
L.A. Angels

For three seasons Mike played

in the Angels' minor leagues.

But early in the 2012 season

the Angels needed an outfielder.

It was Mike's time to shine.

2009

born in
Vineland,
New Jersey

attends high
school in Millville,
New Jersey

drafted by the
L.A. Angels

15

Mike set records as

a MLB rookie for stolen bases

and runs scored. He was

named the American League

Rookie of the Year for 2012.

**1991**
born in
Vineland,
New Jersey

**2007–2009**
attends high
school in Millville,
New Jersey

**2009**
drafted by the
L.A. Angels

**2012**
named
American
League Rookie
of the Year

Fans enjoyed watching

Mike play. They voted him

onto the 2012 American League

All-Star team. He played again

in the 2013 All-Star Game.

**1991**
born in
Vineland,
New Jersey

**2007–2009**
attends high
school in Millville,
New Jersey

**2009**
drafted by the
L.A. Angels

**2012**
named
American
League Rookie
of the Year

**2012**
plays in his
first All-Star
Game

**2013**
plays in
his second
All-Star Game

Mike's third season was his best yet.

He was named the 2014 All-Star

Game's Most Valuable Player.

He also agreed to play for

the Angels for six more years.

| 1991 | 2007–2009 | 2009 | 2012 | 2012 | 2013 | 2014 |
|---|---|---|---|---|---|---|
| born in Vineland, New Jersey | attends high school in Millville, New Jersey | drafted by the L.A. Angels | named American League Rookie of the Year | plays in his first All-Star Game | plays in his second All-Star Game | plays in his third All-Star Game and earns Most Valuable Player title |

# GLOSSARY

**All-Star Game**—a Major League Baseball game played once a year; the teams are made up of baseball's biggest stars

**draft**—an event held for teams to choose new people to play for them

**Little League**—a youth baseball organization with teams throughout the world

**minor league**—a league of teams where players improve their playing skills before joining a major league team

**record**—when something is done better than anyone has ever done it before

**rookie**—a first year player

**season**—the time of year in which MLB baseball games are played

**tee ball**—a beginning level of baseball that allows the batters to swing at a ball placed on a tee

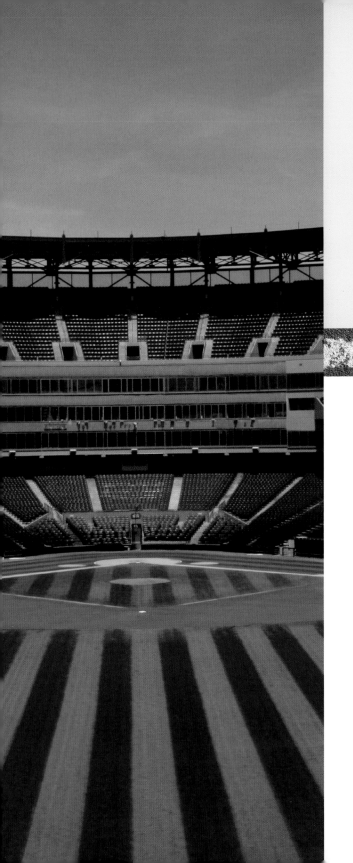

# READ MORE

**Doeden, Matt.** *All About Baseball.* All About Sports. North Mankato, Minn: Capstone Press, 2015.

**Fishman, Jon M.** *Mike Trout.* Amazing Athletes. Minneapolis: Lerner, 2014.

**Gagne, Tammy.** *Mike Trout.* Blue Banner Biographies. Hockessin, Del.: Mitchell Lane Publishers, 2014.

# INTERNET SITES

FactHound offers a safe, fun way to find Internet sites related to this book. All of the sites on FactHound have been researched by our staff.

Here's all you do:

Visit *www.facthound.com*

Type in this code: 9781491462379

Super-cool stuff!

Check out projects, games and lots more at
**www.capstonekids.com**

# CRITICAL THINKING USING THE COMMON CORE

1. Read the text on page 8. Describe why speed would be an important baseball skill. (Integration of Knowledge and Ideas)

2. Mike Trout set high school and MLB records. Use the glossary to describe what a record is. (Craft and Structure)

## INDEX

Word Count: 241
Grade: 1
Early-Intervention Level: 17

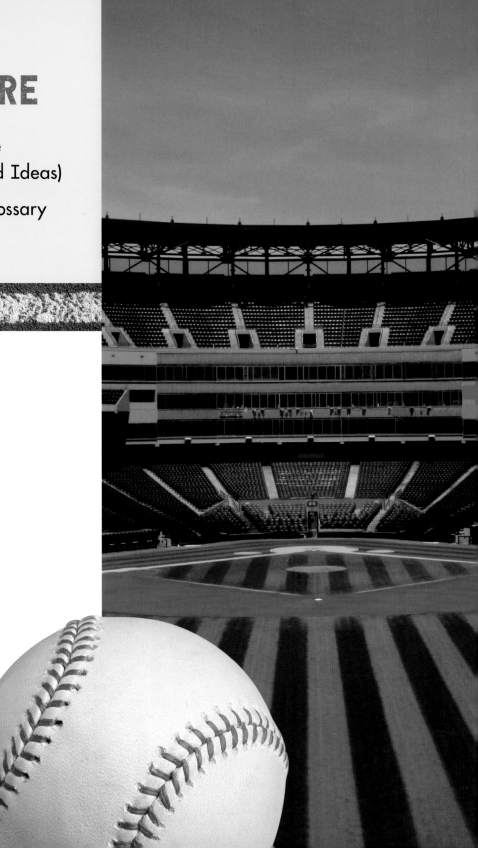